Destroying the Spirit of Limitation

"Developing a Consciousness of Unlimited Potential"

Destroying the Spirit of Limitation

"Developing a Consciousness of Unlimited Potential"

By

Dr. Ronald L. Hamm

*in*POWERu Publishing

Destroying the Spirit of Limitation
Copyright © 2014 by Dr. Ronald L. Hamm

Editor: Tyrrell Brown, Sr.

ISBN: 978-0-9790955-2-8

Printed in USA

Dedication

To my beautiful and loving wife Sonya for your wisdom and support in all that I do. Without you in my life I know I would not be the man I am today. Thank you for pushing me to always strive for and do my best for God. Next to the Lord, you are my most cherished friend. You are an excellent teacher and accomplished author as well as a devoted wife and mother to our children. Thank you for helping me to raise our children to know and honor God. To my children; Ronald, Brynique, Tynesia and Je'Ron, thank you for your love and support.

To the entire Resurrection Life Worship Center International leaders, family and friends, you are amazing and your tireless commitment to the things of God inspires me to continue to reach for the highest level possible. To Tyrrell Brown Sr., thank you for your contribution in editing this book. Your sacrifice, attention to detail and commitment to excellence made it possible to produce a quality book.

To my spiritual parents Bishop I.V. Hilliard and Pastor Bridget Hilliard, thank you for your Godly example and excellence in teaching your sons and daughters to walk in a lifestyle of faith. Thank you for inspiring me to go beyond my limitation. You have blessed my family in ways unimaginable.

Table of Contents

Introduction

After having traveled all across the world, serving in the United States Army for over twenty years, I've had the opportunity to meet people of different cultures and backgrounds. What intrigued me the most is that regardless of their academic accomplishments, social economic status, race or nationality, I have found that most people have not lived a fulfilled life because of limitations and restrictions that have been placed before them. Quite often I've also come into contact with many Christians who are not functioning at their full potential because of their limiting beliefs.

We were all created with purpose. God did not allow us to come into this world without a purpose. Regardless of how you arrived on the planet; planned birth, unplanned birth, rape or incest, you were created to fulfill God's plan and purpose for your life. It is my desire to help the people of God maximize their potential, fulfill their destiny and function at the highest level of purpose in which they were created. As I look at my own life, I can find instances where I allowed myself to be limited or restricted from accomplishing my goals and aspirations.

The road to destiny is always progressive and everything that God creates is always expanding and producing. When God spoke light into existence, it appeared and is still expanding at 186, 000 miles per second. When He created mankind, He gave the instruction to be fruitful and multiply and fill the earth. God also created every living thing with a seed that will continue to reproduce and expand. The universe is still expanding since the first day God spoke its existence. So God is all about multiplication and not subtraction. His desire is for you to go from faith to faith and glory to glory. The spirit of limitation is a force whose purpose is to restrict, resist and restrain you from reaching your destiny. It must be destroyed so that you can fulfill everything that God has for you. The truth is that most of our limitations are in the mind. I want to deal with the complex system of the mind that God gave us to function in this world as partakers of His glory.

The mind consists of three parts; the conscious mind, subconscious mind and conscience mind. The conscience mind houses your core belief system and values. The subconscious mind is the part of your mind that operates automatically when you are not aware or focus on what is at hand. But what I want to focus on is the conscious mind. The conscious mind allows you to be aware of your surroundings.

Chapter One

Revealing the Power of Consciousness

What is Consciousness?

Consciousness is a very powerful thing and if we learn how to illuminate the power of consciousness we will be able to breach every obstacle that lies between us and our destiny. Psychologists have studied consciousness for quite some time. I don't want to get into the deep discussion of what their findings were but the conscious mind, or should I say the state of consciousness, is always shifting with thought. You have the ability to think on past memories, present experiences and also on the future. While reading this book your thoughts can shift to experiences from your past and in the next moment you can think on your desire for the future. This is the power of consciousness. If a person is unconscious they do not have the faculty of thought or the awareness of their surroundings. Only when that person gains consciousness are they able to be aware. When this happens, they have what I'd like to call, situational awareness. Situational awareness is a term I learned years ago while deployed with the United States Army in Bosnia and Herzegovina. It simply means that we were to be cognizant of our surroundings at all times. Making a deliberate effort to pay attention continuously and consistently which could be a matter of life or death. In other words, the instructions were to always be focused and ready to prevent or respond to any situation that may occur.

The Scripture testifies that God is the originator and creator of everything including you and me. Your very existence is found in God and anything that is outside of Him does not exist. I know that might sound a little crazy but what I am simply saying is that there is nothing that exists outside of the creator. When someone enters into existence that means that they enter into a state of awareness or consciousness through the five senses (taste, touch, smell, hearing and seeing).

"For in Him we live, we move, and have our being……" *(Acts 17:28).*

The air that you breathe is inside of you and all around you. In the same way, God is in you, around you and before you. We live in Him, we move in Him and have our identity in Him. Another way to put this is that a fish that is in the ocean is in the water but water is also in the fish. It cannot survive outside of the environment in which it was created to live and thrive. Outside of the water it is helpless and dying but in the water it performs at its highest potential. In the same manner, outside of God we are dying and operating below our full capacity but in Him we will reach our full potential and fulfill our divine purpose that He created us for. Everything that God creates is all part of his overall plan for the universe. Everything in the universe is related but each has been uniquely given a purpose that benefits the overall plan. I don't know about you but it is hard for me to look at the galaxies, solar systems, planets to include the Earth and not believe that there is a God and that He has a plan.

Most of you know the story of Adam and Eve and how they fell from grace in the garden by disobeying God. Adam was instructed by God to eat of every tree in the garden except the tree of the knowledge of good and evil.

6 And when the woman saw that the tree was good for food, and that it was pleasant to the eyes, and a tree to be desired to make one wise, she took of the fruit thereof, and did eat, and gave also unto her husband with her; and he did eat.

⁷ And the eyes of them both were opened, and they knew that they were naked; and they sewed fig leaves together, and made themselves aprons. (Genesis 3:6-7)

In this passage we see that when Adam and Eve disobeyed God and ate of the fruit, their eyes were opened and they knew that they were naked. We know that the scripture is not indicating that they were physically blind before eating but that actually something happened to them; they knew that they were naked. So it is safe to say that they entered into a state of consciousness that they were not in prior to this event. Consciousness in associated with the human condition and the state of mind of an individual is based on their state of consciousness. I don't mean to sound philosophical or professorial, but I do want to lay a foundation for the revelation that God has given me in this book. Consciousness brings you into a state of awareness, a state of reasoning and a place of intelligence that you did not possess before. Adam and Eve were now conscious of their nakedness and they hid themselves, in their own minds, from the presence of God.

What have you done in your past that has caused you to hide yourself from God? The truth is that God has never used perfect people to accomplish His will in the earth. The enemy will use your bad decisions from the past, to restrict and limit you from walking in your destiny. The number one thing that hinders you from moving forward is allowing your past to live rent free in your consciousness. When my son was a little boy, he said something very profound to me that changed my way of thinking for rest of my life. He said, "Dad, did you know that in order to go left you must push to the right, in order to go right you must push left, in order to go down you must push up and in order to go up you must push down". When I heard this, a revelation jumped into my spirit that wherever I resist I will move in the opposite direction. If you want to move forward you must resist the past.

12 Then said he unto me, Fear not, Daniel: for from the first day that thou didst set thine heart to understand, and to chasten thyself before thy God, thy words were heard, and I am come for thy words.

13 But the prince of the kingdom of Persia withstood me one and twenty days: but, lo, Michael, one of the chief princes, came to help me; and I remained there with the kings of Persia. (Daniel 10:12-13)

I have entitled this book, **"Destroying the Spirit of Limitation"**, because I believe that limitations and are spirits. In the above scripture, Daniel had been praying to God on behalf of the nation of Israel for over three weeks but he had not received an answer. The angel then appeared unto Daniel and said unto him that he heard him from the first time he began to pray but, in the spirit realm, he was restricted for twenty-one days from answering his words because of the prince of the kingdom of Persia that withheld him. It was not until the archangel Michael came to help him that the restricting spirit was overcome. There are demonic forces assigned to your life whose sole purpose is to restrict you and prevent you from operating at your full potential and capacity in Christ Jesus. Whenever you decide to move for God, there will always be demonic and satanic opposition assigned to block that move. Most of the opposition is not external but within your own mind.

Growing up in Montgomery, Alabama, in the 70s and 80s, I can remember the remnants of the civil right struggles and the social economic woes of African Americans. What seemed normal at the time, I later realized, was due to social conditioning and the mindset of the people. I didn't realize, at the time, that my conscience was being shaped with false limitations. I remember wondering why was it that most of the black people resided on the worse side of the city and lived in sub-standard homes. My brother and I would ride our bikes on the upper class side of town and look at the big beautiful homes with perfectly manicured lawns and swimming pools. The accepted belief of the people in my family and the people around me was, that's just the way things were and it would never change because some people were destined to be poor. Even from the pulpit the message was that wealth and riches would be ours when we die and go to heaven: Then and only then would we be able to walk the streets of gold. The preacher said that in heaven, there would be no more sickness, no crying, no more heartaches and pain. I remember thinking to myself, at age fourteen, why do we have to wait until we get to heaven to live a wonderful life. I was not in a position to change my circumstances but it was the beginning of a mind shift.

And there we saw the giants, the sons of Anak, which come of the giants: and we were in our own sight as **grasshoppers***, and so we were in their sight. (Numbers 13:33)*

My environment was a negative one. The common vernacular of the people around me was always negative and faithless. My own thoughts were that certain things were not possible for certain types of people. In the scripture above, we see that after Moses sent spies into the Promised Land, the report came back by the majority that there were giants in the land and the giants perceived them to be as grasshoppers. This scripture indicates that the limitation came from within and not from the giants. Whenever you perceive your problem to be greater than you, then and only then can you be limited by it.

Identifying Your Limitations

When something is broken it has the possibility of being restored, revived or reconstructed. However when something is destroyed it cannot be fixed, repaired, revitalized or invigorated. When an automobile is involved in a collision, it is either damaged or totaled. To be totaled means that the car cannot be restored back to functional capacity. I want to show you how to destroy the spirit of limitations in your life and not just break them. Limits are defined as the final, utmost, or furthest boundary. It means to restrict by or as if by establishing boundaries. Limitation causes you to be hampered in activity, growth, and effectiveness. They are set in your life by the enemy to restrain you from reaching your full God given potential thereby causing you to delay the plan of God for your life and ultimately cause you to abort your destiny.

From a Child's Perspective

Children are amazing to me. They will not hesitant. From a child's perspective there are no limitations, difficulties or restrictions. When my children were growing up, they did not want help performing certain tasks. I would try to open something for them but they would tell me, "Let me do it daddy". There was nothing that they did not feel they could do. When I was about ten years old, I remember that once I had a vision of digging a tunnel to my cousin's house which was about two blocks from my house. As I begin digging I soon found out that it was not as easy as I thought it would be. I soon realized that there were some limitations that I had not thought of. My vision was possible but I did not have the proper tools to complete the task. I kept convincing myself that one day I would do it when I had the proper resources and time. I was limited by my resources, limited by my experience and limited by my thoughts. The point that I want to make is that my vision was not impossible but there were certain physical, mental and time restrictions that I had to deal with through the process.

I remember when my wife and I decided to purchase our first home. My mental thought was that it was very hard to purchase a home and that the bank would not approve the loan for the mortgage. The reason why I thought this way was because I had never seen anyone purchase a home when I was growing up. It was my wife that motivated me and encouraged me to pursue purchasing the new home. If it had not been for her, my mental limitations would have stopped me from purchasing it. The way that we think is a result of our environment, credible people in our lives, things that we hear on repetitious basis and life experiences. As I began to mature in age, I realized that there were mental barriers that I had allowed to set in my mind that limited me from reaching my highest potential.

I believe that everyone has a desire for greater but sometimes they allow their thoughts to limit them. I want to encourage you to move past your limitations and walk in a place of abundance and great success in which God as created you to do.

Limitations are learned

Limitations are not automatic they are taught to us by our environment, experiences, and others around that we hold to be credible. My spiritual father always tells me that more is caught than taught. What he was saying was that you can learn more by observing the actions of others than you can through systematic instruction. The more you watch a person, the more you pick you their values and wisdom. That is why it is important who you hang around. When you hang around dirt you began to speak dirt. If you want to change your situation, you must change your environment. You are the sum total of the five closest friends or associates in your life. If they have limiting beliefs then most likely you will also develop limiting beliefs. If you observe successful people you will most likely do what they did to become successful.

All limitations can be broken.

Boundaries are placed before you to keep you within certain parameters or borders. When boundaries are in place you have limited access into certain places. Have you ever seen a sign that says, Do not enter, authorized personnel only? This simply means that only authorized personnel can exceed or bypass the boundaries that have been put into place. If you want to enter then you must have the credentials to gain access. Every obstacle in your life can be overcome. Every circumstance can be reversed, every boundary can be exceeded and every limitation can be broken. For every policy there is always an exception to policy. Nothing is absolute.

"Consciousness is associated with the human condition and the state of mind of an individual is based on their state of consciousness."

Chapter Two

Reinforcing Faith That Opens Doors

Doors are created for the purpose of allowing or denying access to certain areas. The first door to be opened for you was the door of your mother's womb. When you were born into this world you enter into a new realm of possibility, no longer restricted by the womb.

Because it shut not up the doors of my mother's womb, nor hid sorrow from mine eyes. (Job 3:10)

Throughout your life you will encounter many doors. Some will be physical and some spiritual. But what is common about both is that they are gateways that mark an entrance or exit from one place or state to another. Have you ever wondered why God close some doors and open others? In God's sovereign wisdom, grace and love, He is able to lead us to what is best for us.

In our society, today many people seek knowledge and direction outside of God using palm readers and physics. Only God knows what is best for us in the short run and for eternity. God has the ability to move in and out of time to move obstacles and barriers to your destiny. For example, if you have a situation on Monday that need to be fixed by Wednesday, God can step out of Monday and move into Wednesday and fix your situation and then step back into Monday and tell you to just be obedient and receive your blessing.

When the Holy Spirit prohibited Paul and Timothy from preaching in Asia they believed God would open a better door to them. Do not get discouraged when you get rejected for a specific job, a certain relationship or a promotion. Trust God, in the process, to open up a better opportunity for you. If we learn to rest and wait on God, the Spirit will reveal the next pathway. Do not get anxious, angry or frustrated when the doors do not open immediately. Many times God will say no to certain prayers in order to direct us to roads that will lead to greater accomplishments. Ask the Lord to give you patience and do not get discouraged when your prayerful desires are not being met. Do not be afraid to have a few doors slammed in your face before finding the best one. Ask the Lord to give you the courage, tenacity and toughness to overcome rejection and exhibit a resilient attitude in your pursuit of God's best. God uses closed doors to open up bigger and better ones for us down the road. I want to talk about four types of doors; prison doors, proximity doors, programmed doors and personal doors.

Prison Doors

As I mentioned earlier, doors are barriers that either allow access or deny access. Prison doors are designed to keep you in a place of bondage. Prison is a place of confinement and restriction. When a person is in prison they cannot enjoy the pleasures of freedom. It is a place of uncertainty, danger and confusion. Movement is restricted and opportunity is limited.

And suddenly there was a great earthquake, so that the foundations of the prison were shaken: and immediately all the doors were opened, and every one's bands were loosed.(Acts 16:26)

In Acts chapter 16, the apostle Paul and Silas find themselves locked behind prison doors. As they begin to sing hymns and pray, an earthquake shook the foundation, the chains fell off and the doors of the prison were opened. A physical prison restricts the body but there are also mental prisons that restrict the mind. It is possible to be physically free but mentally and spiritually incarcerated. Physical doors can be unlocked with keys or codes but mental and spiritual prisons can only be unlocked my spiritual means. When Paul and Silas were restricted physically they understood that their spirits were free. They began to sing praises unto God which caused God to respond to their physical condition. Many people, however, are incarcerated or imprisoned in their minds. Before a person can be totally free, physically, they must be free in their mind. The Scripture tells us that whatever a man thinks in his heart, so is he. The greatest hindrance to your success is your state of mind. The desire of the devil is to keep your mind locked in the past so that you will not have faith for the future. Depression is one of the greatest weapons of the enemy. Depression is a condition of the emotions of an individual which causes sadness and withdrawal over a prolonged period of time. There are many believers preaching in the pulpit, singing on the praise team, and greeting at the door that are caught up in the prison of depression. Moses was the depressed leader of the children of Israel. Every time he turned around, they griped about something. "We need water." "We are starving." "We want food, and we are tired of manna." If you were surrounded by a bunch of chronic complainers it would be hard not to be depressed.

Job was depressed. He lost everything, and then cursed the day he was born:

"Why did I not perish at birth, and die as I came from the womb?.... I have no peace, no quietness; I have no rest, but only turmoil." (Job 3:11, 3:26)

David was depressed:

"Be merciful to me, Lord, for I am faint; O Lord, heal me, for my bones are in agony. My soul is in anguish. How long, O Lord, how long?.... I am writing worn out from groaning; all night long I flood my bed with weeping and drench my couch with tears." (Psalm 6:2-3, 6)

The apostle Paul was depressed. In II Corinthians 12 we are told that Paul was given a thorn in the flesh to perhaps keep him humble. Paul said it was a messenger of satan, to torment him. So we see many in the scripture who fell into the prison of depression but they overcame.

Five Steps for Deal with the Prison of Depression

1. Take off the Mask.

Many times we put on a mask in order to cover up how we really feel because we don't want others to know. There are pastors that are committing suicide because they are depressed. In many cases, the congregations never saw it coming because they had learned to cover it up. If everything is not okay, stop acting as though it is.

2. Pray an Honest Prayer to God.

When we pray to God we are not informing him of anything because he is omniscient. He knows everything about you even the number of hairs on your head. When I say pray an honest prayer to God, essentially what I am saying is pray from a place of honesty within you. Acknowledge the pain and discomfort that you are experiencing, before God.

3. Release all Bitterness and Blame.

Bitterness and blame are the chains that keep you bound in the prison of depression. You must release those that have hurt you, hindered you, and harass you in order to move forward. If you are still holding on to things from the past then you are in a spiritual prison. Chances are the people that hurt you have forgotten about it and move on but you are still stuck in prison. I challenge you to release yourself, release them and move into your destiny.

4. Receive Strength From God.

And he said unto me, My grace is sufficient for thee: for my strength is made perfect in weakness. Most gladly therefore will I rather glory in my infirmities, that the power of Christ may rest upon me (2 Corinthians 12:9)

You must realize that God is your strength. At your weakest moment His strength and made perfect in you. If you can handle things with your own strength then there is no need for God. God shows up when you can no longer handle it.

5. Move Forward in God's strength.

Once you receive the strength of God, move forward into your destiny. Depression can only set in when we take God out of the equation. When you receive strength from God move forward with Him and your strength will never run out.

I believe that God is shaking the very foundations of the earth and causing prison doors the open for His people.

Proximity Doors

Have you ever been to the supermarket or department store and observed the doors opening automatically? When you stepped in proximity of the door the sensors recognized you and it opened for you because you were at the right place at the right time. Proximity is defined as nearness in space or time. There are some blessings that will come to you or doors that will open for you just because you are in proximity of them. There is a difference in proximity and presence. It is possible to be in proximity of a person but not in their presence. There is an old song that I remember growing up that said, "Your body is here with me but your mind is on the other side of town." To be in proximity of God is to be near Him but to be in His presence is to be totally focused on Him. If you associate yourself with blessed people then the overflow of their blessings can fall on you. Likewise, I believe that some people around you are blessed just because they are in proximity of you but there are greater blessing that comes from being in the presence of God. One of the attributes of God is that He is omnipresent which means that He is everywhere at the same time. It is not possible to go anywhere to get away from Him. To be out of God's presence is to be uncovered and away from place of blessings. To be in His presence is to walk in obedience and reverence to Him.

Programmed Doors

Bring ye all the tithes into the storehouse, that there may be meat in mine house, and prove me now herewith, saith the Lord of hosts, if I will not open you the windows of heaven, and pour you out a blessing, that there shall not be room enough to receive it. (Malachi 3:10)

Programmed doors are doors that require certain conditions to open. A specific code or instruction is needed to unlock these types of doors. In the above scripture the prophet Malachi tells us that if we bring the tithe into the house of God, He will open up the windows, or shall we say doors, of heaven and poor out a blessing that cannot be contained. So we can safely say that the code needed to open the windows of heaven is the bringing of the tithe. This is a conditional promise that was established by God for those that desire to walk under an open heaven. If you fail to use the code it will restrict you from experiencing the blessings. If you want to get beyond limited blessings, begin to tithe into the house of God and receive from God's unlimited supply.

Personal Doors

*Lift up your heads, O ye gates; even lift them up, ye everlasting **doors**; and the King of glory shall come in. (**Psalm 24:9**)*

Personal doors are doors that you are able to open for yourself. What we must understand is that the doors that you open will affect not only you but your whole household. The Scriptures says that a good man leaves an inheritance to his children's children. Inheritance in and the context of this book refers to blessing. I believe that it is the responsibility of every man to ensure that the next generation is taking care of. You must understand that if a man can open the door to generational blessings for his family then he can also open the door to generational curses. God said he would judge some sins to the third and fourth generation. So it is important to choose the correct personal doors that you open for your family and the generations to come.

Over the years, I have counseled with many men who did not realize that generational curses had been released through their family by the grandfather or great-grandfather. The way they think about money or prosperity, how to treat women, or how to be a father had been passed down through generations. Alcoholism, drug abuse, depression and fear were their inheritance. In each case I informed them that they had the power to close the door and cancel the curses that had been released over them. Then I encouraged them to open new doors of opportunity, success, prosperity and healing that will reach into the generations to come. Generational curses can cause limitations and restrictions in your life but the good news is that it can be destroyed. The scripture above informs us that we are everlasting doors. Close the door to curses and opened the door to blessings. You are everlasting doors, meaning that regardless if you are aware or not you are always opening or closing doors that affect generations. I declare and decree that every generational curse is broken in your life and you are about to step into a new place of tremendous blessings in Christ Jesus!

Unlock the **prison doors** with praise and adoration until Almighty God. Get in the right position and allow every **proximity door** to be opened in your life. Obey God's word and His conditional promises and receive the code that will open every **programmed door** that stands between you and your blessing. And finally, it is your responsibility to open the right **personal doors** that will affect the generations to come.

"Many times God will say no to certain prayers in order to direct us to roads that will lead to greater accomplishments."

Chapter Three

Relieving Your Past

And when he was come out of the ship, immediately there met him out of the tombs a man with an unclean spirit,

³ Who had his dwelling among the tombs; and no man could bind him, no, not with chains:

⁴ Because that he had been often bound with fetters and chains, and the chains had been plucked asunder by him, and the fetters broken in pieces: neither could any man tame him.

⁵ And always, night and day, he was in the mountains, and in the tombs, crying, and cutting himself with stones. (Mark5:2-5)

One of the greatest roadblocks to reaching your destiny is to dwell in the past. In this passage of Scripture there was a man who was living in a cemetery out of his mind. He could not be bound with chains or fetters because the strength of his condition was holding him strong.

This man was in a deep state of depression crying day and night. Not only was he crying but he was bringing physical harm to himself by cutting himself with stones. This man was also created with purpose and his purpose was not to be restricted or limited to hanging out in the cemetery. The Scripture does not indicate how he ended up in the cemetery out of his mind but I would assume that something drastic and devastating happened in his life that caused this limitation to be placed on him. As I stated before, I believe that limitation is a spirit whose sole purpose is to derail us from reaching our purpose and destiny in Christ Jesus.

The cemetery or the tomb is a place for those whose lives are in the past. The people that are there once walked the earth but now they are restricted to the grave. There is no life in the cemetery only a place of what used to be. This man was dwelling in the past; depressed, emotional, delusional, and suicidal but there was still a destiny set before him. I encourage you to get your bibles and finish reading this story. You will find that there were demonic spirits inside of the man that limited him and restricted him to the tomb. It was not until Jesus showed up, that he was released from the spirit of limitation, to walk into his destiny. So, as you see, your past can cause you to be limited. There are many people today that are still bound by what happened to them years ago. Some were molested, some was emotionally abused, some were abandoned, and some were not loved by the ones who should have loved them. If you are in one of those categories I employ you now to forgive those that hurt you and release yourself from the bondage of your past. It is the goal of the enemy to always remind you of the hurt and pain that you have endured but God will give you the peace that surpasses all understanding to guard your hearts and minds in Christ Jesus. If you refuse to let your past go, you are just like the man in the tomb; hanging out in the cemetery.

When I was four years old, my mother, died at a young age and left behind ten children that needed a home. As a result of that, several of us were adopted by families throughout the city. Throughout the years, in my adopted family, I would notice that there were times when my brother and I were not treated the same as the other children in that family. We would always receive hand me downs and used things but the nephews and nieces would get new things. My brother and I would always discuss how we felt but never thought we could do anything about it. I grew up with abandonment issues not understanding why my mother died in the first place and left us alone. For years I was angry at her and the family that adopted us because I did not feel the love of a nurturing mother. As a result I grew up with the need to be needed and loved. This led me to a life being dependent on others to make me happy. I became a victim and limited myself from achieving goals that I had set because I had nobody to help me. I became victimized by my past and began to dwell there. I eventually realized that I would always be limited if I look to people rather than God.

I press toward the mark for the prize of the high calling of God in Christ Jesus. (Philippians 3:14)

Memories are past experiences painted on the canvas of your mind. Dreams and visions are future insights impressed into your imagination. The past and future are not real to most people but I beg to differ. The Apostle Paul encourages us to forget the past and stretch towards the future.

We've all experienced things in our past that we regret. It takes many forms like regret over marital situations, imagining how much happier your life would have been if you had married someone else, regret over divorce, regret over broken relationships of all kinds, regret over mistakes you made raising your kids, regret over bad career moves, regret over missed business opportunities, poor vocational choices and in general, regret over all kinds of sins and the consequences of those sins. One thing for sure is that you can never go back into your past and change anything but you can leave your past behind and stretch into your future. The good news is that we don't have to be paralyzed by regret and we don't have to let our past rob us of the joy and hope that God has promised us as our birthright in Christ. Jesus said, *"I came that they may have life, and have it abundantly." John 10:10.* I don't know about you but I want the life that Jesus came to give me.

Say this confession:

I declare and decree that from this day forth I will not be limited by my past but I choose to seek God's plan for my life and walk into my future in Jesus' name.

Chapter Four

Releasing Your Present

25 And a certain woman, which had an issue of blood twelve years,

26 And had suffered many things of many physicians, and had spent all that she had, and was nothing bettered, but rather grew worse,

27 When she had heard of Jesus, came in the press behind, and touched his garment.

28 For she said, If I may touch but his clothes, I shall be whole.

29 And straightway the fountain of her blood was dried up; and she felt in her body that she was healed of that plague. (Mark 5:25-29)

The conscious mind is always operating in one of three realms; the past, the present and the future. The past and the future have one thing in common and that is that they both are mental pictures or images. The present is always happening now. Not only do your past cause limitations in your life, but you can also be limited in the present. The present acquires sensory perception and verification in the natural realm. What I mean is that in the natural realm we've been conditioned to rely on our sense of smell, touch, taste, hearing and seeing. Every sin is associated with these senses and become a gateway for demonic activity in our lives if we are not in control of them. You need to understand that if faith can come by hearing then so can doubt. It is important to always be in communion with the Holy Spirit and not distracted by what is going on with you and around you in the present.

The woman in the previous scripture had an issue of blood for twelve long years. Her menstrual cycle had not stopped flowing for twelve years. When you read the full background of this passage you will find that she had spent all of her money and possessions on medical treatment but could not be help by anyone. Because of her condition, she found herself alienated from the rest of society because the tradition was that a woman was considered unclean during this time and could not be in public. Her body was weak and her mind was exhausted. Let's focus on this issue for a moment because there is more to it than meets the eye. Not only was she alienated from society, she was also in a state of no productivity. When a woman is experiencing her menstrual cycle, her body is not able to produce the eggs necessary to conceive a child. So for twelve years this woman could not receive the blessings and breakthrough that she needed to manifest in her life. Every day, this condition was a present reality and reminded her of her limitation. Imagine having to dealing with the flow of blood day after day, a flow that would hinder your progress and block the manifestation of the blessing of God in your life. This woman realized that the only way to fix her present limitation was through the power of God operating through our Lord and Savior, Jesus Christ. She recognized that she was in a state of limitation and so she decided to do something about it. That day, after her miracle, the very thing that was limiting her was dried up and she began to walk in her blessing.

What's your Issue?

Most of the time when you ask someone how they are doing, they will reply, "fine" because we have been conditioned to hold things in or put on a mask. Sin cannot be seen, only the effects of it. It is spiritual in its origin. There are many people that have issues and situations in their lives that hinders the blessings of God from manifesting in their lives. I want to ask you a question, What's your issue? What is your flow that blocks the blessings from coming into your life? I believe that if you are not seeing manifestation in your life it is because of the things that you are allowing to hold you back. The woman had a physical issue but there are many people that have mental, spiritual and psychological issues active in their lives that hinder their breakthrough.

Wherefore seeing we also are compassed about with so great a cloud of witnesses, let us lay aside every weight, and the sin which doth so easily beset us, and let us run with patience the race that is set before us, Hebrews (12:1-3)

In the world that we live in, the opportunity for sin to enter in is not difficult. Computers, commercials, cartoons, television shows, video games and billboards, you name it, are full of sex, violence and greed. Not only are these things plaguing our society but they have somehow crept into the church.

Sin actually means to miss the mark. It was an archery term used to identify when someone missed the target. Sin is also synonymous with disobedience and rebellion against the Word of God. How can you expect God to supernaturally bless you when you are in a state of disobedience and rebellion? There are some blessings that will fall on everyone but there are others that require obedience. Everyone that is alive enjoys the blessing of air, water and sunshine but if you want to receive the promises of God you must walk in obedience and submission.

God wants to bless you now and in the future. I don't believe that we are supposed to wait until we get to heaven to experience the blessings and favor of God. When I was growing up I would always here the church people say that one day I'm going to put on my long white robe, golden slippers and golden crown and walk around heaven all day. The problem with that is that I would have to die before I walk in my blessed state. On the other hand, they would say we are blessed in the city and in the field, blessed coming in and going out. I didn't understand that because they were contradicting themselves.

I believe that God want us to be prosperous, healed and blessed NOW! In the Lord's Prayer it says that the kingdom has come on earth as it is in heaven. That means that the benefits of the kingdom is on the earth and we should walk in the highest quality of life. In John 10:10, Jesus says that he came to bring us an abundant life. Don't let sin hinder you from a better quality of life in God.

The scripture says that we should lay aside every weight and sin that so easily beset us. The word beset means to restrict or limit. I declare that sin, sickness and disease are not welcomed in your life.

The first step in laying aside sin is to admit that you are in sin. You cannot be freed from sin if you don't believe what you are doing is wrong. Secondly, you must cease to obey the spirit of the sin whose purpose is to bring death to you. Sin originates as a thought which then causes actions. The scripture say that you must lay it aside. No one can release you from sin except you. I don't care how many hands are laid on you or how many prophetic words are spoken over you, sin will only go if you let it go. Make a decision to put it down just as you made a decision to pick it up.

Metaphorically speaking, the woman's blood flow is comparable to the sin in your life. Both will block you from experiencing God's best for you. I am always checking myself to make sure that I am not walking in sin and disobedience.

"Every sin is associated with your senses and becomes a gateway for demonic activity in your life if you are not in control of them."

Chapter Five

Revoking Your Fears

For God hath not given us the spirit of fear; but of power, and of love, and of a sound mind. (2 Timothy 1:7)

There is a mechanism deep inside of each of us that alerts us when there is potential danger or possible harm near. This inward emotion is cultivated and nurtured as we grow up. Fear is an emotion that can cripple you and cause you to hesitation when action is required. As a former soldier, I like to use military comparisons to get my point across. Fears are like land mines that are buried and cannot be seen. Trying to navigate through a mind field can be very frightening because at any time you could step on a mine and lose your life. The scripture says that God did not give us the spirit of fear. We see in this passage that fear is called a spirit. It is always associated with the spirit of limitation. This is not a spirit that God gave to us therefore; don't hold on to that which does not belong to you. The scripture goes on to say that God gave us the spirit of power, love and sound mind. There is a spirit connected to every emotion, therefore we must intentionally and purposely allow the Holy Spirit to occupy our minds. The emotion of fear cannot occupy the same space or realm as courage. Fear can only raise its head where there is an absence of courage. God told Joshua in *Joshua 1:9 (NLT)*: *"I command you be strong and courageous. Do not be afraid or discouraged. For the Lord your God is with you wherever you go."* An awareness of God's presence with you will always eradicate the effects of fear within you. It is like a child being with its father; the child will be free of fear. Fear keeps us from living life to its fullest and from being the people of God that He designed us to become. Let's consider four areas of fear that limit progress, productivity and prosperity.

1.   Fear of the unknown

Some people are maximum performers when operating in their comfort zone but when they are placed in a new environment they cannot function effectively because of the spirit of fear. Fear will keep you at your current status, but if you want something new you must do something new. If you keep doing the same thing you will get the same thing. Have you ever thought about why some people have a fear of height? It is mainly because of their perspective. Fear is always a matter of perspective. If you place both of your hands before your face, with one closer than the other, the one closer to your face will appear larger. This is only because of the distance or perspective from which you are looking. You may fear the unknown because you are looking at the situation from your own perspective and not God's perspective. God knows all and He sees all; therefore trust Him and evict the spirit of fear from your thoughts. To combat the fear of the unknown you must become one with God who knows all things. Throughout my military career I was deployed into several war zones and combat theaters. I learned not to be in fear but to trust in God who sees me as well as my enemies. I remember my mother saying, "God sits high and looks low". She meant that God perspective is higher than ours and He sees everything.

Yea, though I walk through the valley of the shadow of death, I will fear no evil: for thou art with me; thy rod and thy staff they comfort me. **(***Psalm 23:4***)**

We can see in this passage that fear cannot be in the same space with God. David said that no matter how bad things seemed, He had no fear because God was with him. God is above all of your circumstances and situations. When you were in the valley, God was there with you and He was also with you during your mountain top experience.

When I was seeking God for a deeper understanding of the call that He had on my life as an Apostle, I received a vision that put things into perspective for me. I did not know what to do or what was ahead for me with the new mandate but I ask God to reveal my purpose and destiny to me. Against all odds, we had just built a church and then I got a new assignment.

In my vision, I was standing in the parking lot of our church and God asked me, "What do you see?" I said, God I see the building and sanctuary and the church being filled with souls. As I continued to rise higher in the air, He asked again, "What do you see?" I said, "I see the city". Again He asked and my response was, "I see the State". Then He asked again and my response was, "I see the United States of America". After a while I was in outer space looking at the earth and God Said, "What do you see?" I replied, "God I see the continents". Then He said to me, "That's what I called you to." I was being called to go to the nations to teach and train pastors and leaders for the work of God's kingdom. Some ministers are called to the local church but I was called to nations. I would have been satisfied being the pastor of a local congregation but God had a plan for my life. Because of my faith in God I will never allow fear to stop me from reaching my God ordained destiny.

When my youngest daughter was a little girl, my wife and I took her to a toy store in Germany and told her that she could have whatever she wanted. She began to select toys on the bottom shelves that cost only a few dollars. She was excited to get them but that was all she could see from her perspective. I was six feet, three inches tall looking at more expensive and quality toys on the top shelves. I picked her up in my arms and when she saw the toys on the top shelf she was more excited. As long as she was on the floor she could only see things from her perspective. When I lifted her up she could see from her father's perspective. God always sees greater for us because His perspective is eternal.

2.   Fear of failure

In every way we're troubled but not crushed, frustrated but not in despair, persecuted but not abandoned, struck down but not destroyed. We are always carrying around the death of Jesus in our bodies, so that the life of Jesus may be clearly shown in our bodies. (2 Corinthians 4:8-10)

There will be many times in your life when you will experience failures and setbacks. Though they may seem to weigh heavy on you, you will not be destroyed. One of the greatest inventors of all times, Thomas Edison, said that before he found the right filament for the light bulb he failed thousands of times. He went on to say that failure was an educational process because he learned thousands of ways not to do it. The Wright brothers tried to create an airplane that could fly but failed at it many times. But because of their tenacity and commitment, they went on to achieve their goal. If Edison would have quit after the first failure, we would not have the light bulb today. If the Wright brothers had given up, we would not have the airplane today. There are some things that you can only learn though failure. Fear of failure causes many people never to start, or try anything that is not completely safe. We need to realize that our failure is not the end but the beginning of an education.

"Many of life's failures are people who did not realize how close they were to success when they gave up."

Thomas Edison

Unforgiveness, anger and bitterness can be the roadblock to your victory in life if you don't learn how to handle failures. I believe that failure has a purpose in your experiences to teach you how to be humble and meek. The bible is filled with people who failed and made bad choices. Most of the people that God used to change the world were people that would not meet your approval. It is funny how people will always remember your failures but forget about your success. God did not make a mistake when he made you. He knows what you will do even before you do it. So He is not surprised by your failures. As a matter of fact, in spite of your failures, He still calls you, anoints you and gives you a purpose and destiny.

There are six steps that I want to share with you that will help you to move past your fear of failure.

Determine what went wrong.

When a person fail or take the wrong course of action, they are fully aware of why it happened most of the time. Failure is usually birth out of poor choices and bad decision making. However this is not always the case. At various times of our lives we all experience different types of failure. Some failures are out of our control. Some failures are due to ignorance or not knowing. Every battle will not be a success in your eyes but remember that the battle is already won. You must understand that if someone else can pass a test then it is also possible for you.

Develop a strategy.

After you have identified what you did wrong the next step is to develop a strategy to succeed. I've heard many times that if you fail to plan, you plan to fail. This is a true statement. A lack of prior planning most likely will lead to failure. To be successful you must develop a strategy to succeed. Frustration is always a sign that you do not have a good plan or that the present one is not working.. Poor planning will lead to poor decision making which ultimately leads to failure. A student must plan to research and study if he or she expects to pass an examination. If you want to enter into a place of wholeness and prosperity you cannot expect it to show up without having a plan. The enemy of your soul has many plans and tricks up his sleeve to knock you off course and put limitations on you. But God has a plan to prosper you and bring you to a desired outcome.

Move forward.

It is of the Lord's **mercies** *that we* **are** *not consumed, because his compassions fail not. They* **are new** *every morning: great is thy faithfulness. (Lamentations 3:22-23).*

After you develop a plan, your strategy for success, you must then move forward and implement your strategy.

"If you can't fly, then run, if you can't run, then walk, if you can't walk, then crawl, but whatever you do, you have to keep moving forward."

Martin Luther King, Jr.

Isn't it great that every day God gives you another twenty-four hours to start over? He gives you another opportunity to move past your failures and get free from the bondage of limitations. It is time to intentionally develop a prayerfully thought out plan for your success.

3. Fear of success

*This book of the law shall not depart out of thy mouth; but thou shalt meditate therein day and night, that thou mayest observe to do according to all that is written therein: for then thou shalt make thy way prosperous, and then thou shalt have **good success**. (Joshua 1:8)*

At the beginning of this book, I discussed the three parts of the mind; conscious, subconscious and conscience. To be conscious is to be aware and to be unconscious is to be unaware. The truth is that most people with a fear of success are not even aware that they have it. If you find yourself not accomplishing short-term or long-term goals you may be suffering from the fear of success. The Bible says that God knows the plan that he has for you, thoughts of peace and not of evil to give you an expected end. His plan does not include failure. God did not create you be a failure but to succeed. To conquer fear you must cause fear to fear you.

I believe that no one wants to fail, and I also believe that there are some people who are afraid of success. In the above Scripture, God is speaking to Joshua and gives him the keys to success. He tells Joshua to meditate in His instructions day and night and follow them, and he will have good success which will also bring about prosperity. The revelation I received from the scripture is that success brings us prosperity. One of the reasons that the enemy does not want God's people to be successful is because he doesn't want us to become prosperous.

Most people prefer to stay in their comfort zones and refrain from experiencing change in their lives. When you are accustomed to doing something repetitiously it may become difficult to change. Advancement only comes to those that are willing to change and to those who get out of their comfortable places.

Symptoms of Fear of Success

If you experience the following thoughts or fears, you might have a fear of success on some level:

- You feel guilty about any success you have, no matter how small, because your friends, family, or co-workers haven't had the same success.
- You do not tell others about your aspirations and accomplishments.
- You avoid or procrastinate on big projects, especially projects that could lead to recognition.
- You frequently compromise your own goals or agenda to avoid conflict in a group, or even conflict within your family.

- You self-sabotage your work or dreams by convincing yourself that you're not good cnough to achieve them.

- You feel, subconsciously, that you don't deserve to enjoy success in your life.

- You believe that if you do achieve success, you won't be able to sustain it. Eventually you'll fail, and end up back in a worse place than where you started. So you think, "Why bother?"

Causes of Fear of Success

Fear of success has several possible causes:

- We fear what success will bring – for example, loneliness, new enemies, being isolated from our family, longer working hours, or being asked for favors or money.

- We fear that the higher we climb in life, the further we're going to fall when we make a mistake.

- We fear the added work, responsibilities, or criticism that we'll face.

- We fear that our relationships will suffer when we become successful. Our friends and family will react with jealousy and cynicism, and we'll lose the ones we love.

- We fear that accomplishing our goals, and realizing that we have the power to be successful, may actually cause an intense regret that we didn't act sooner.

Often a fear of success is accompanied by a lack of confidence. Developing and strengthening your personal confidence goes a long way in reducing and eliminating a fear of success. When your confidence is strong you trust in God to help you deal with changes that success brings.

4.   Fear of Rejection

"Blessed are you when men hate you, when they exclude you and insult you and reject your name as evil, because of the Son of Man. Rejoice in that day and leap for joy, because great is your reward in heaven". (Luke 6:22-23a).

The dictionary defines rejection as the refusal to have, to take, to recognize, or accept (someone or something).

My first experience with rejection happened when I was five years old. My mother died while giving birth at the age of thirty-nine. Even though I was very young, at the time, I still remember some of the events that happened. My mother had a total of ten living children when she died. We were all separated and adopted into other families. I remember growing up wondering why my aunt had not taken some of her sister's children. I felt as if my mother left us and our family did not want us. I later found out that my aunt did indeed take in my younger brother and sister. The spirit of rejection caused me to go through most of my life expecting to be rejected by everyone in my life. Whether it was not being picked for the basketball team by the kids in the neighborhood, not making the football team, getting into the college of choice, not getting the job hoped for, not getting approved for a loan or a credit card, one way or another, we all have experienced rejection and felt the effects that it brings with it. Remember the dictionary definition of rejection is the refusal to have, to take, to recognize, or accept (someone or something). So rejection is a part of life that affects each of us at some point or another and it is not limited to only one instance. The important thing that we need to learn is not so much how to avoid rejection but how to avoid the traps that rejection sets in your life that will ultimately cause you to be in a state of limitation.

Now let us address the fear of rejection. Some people spend too much time worrying about what someone else thinks about them and too little time thinking about what God says about them. Fear of rejection will cause you to be afraid to do anything that could draw criticism or give someone a chance to laugh at you.

The previous scripture says that you are blessed when men reject you. Remember that Jesus knows how it feels to be rejected.

For God so loved the world that he gave his one and only son, that whoever believes in him shall not perish but have eternal life (John 3:16).

You are included in the "whosoever" category. God loved the world so much that He gave His only Son, Jesus Christ, to die as a sacrifice for your sins. If you accept Jesus as your Lord and Savior, you will have eternal life.

"He who listens to you listens to me; he who rejects you rejects me; but he who rejects me rejects him who sent me" (Luke 10:16).

When someone rejects you for Jesus' sake, they are also rejecting God. Rejection gives you a sense of loss and creates a deficit in your conscience. It causes you to feel offended. Denial is the most common response when you are rejected. To deny that something happened will not cause the situation to go away but it becomes a mechanism of self-defense. We deny that something unpleasant is happening because the reality is too painful to deal with. You need to understand that you can only be affected by the rejection of those with whom you need approval. Don't allow yourself to be limited because you are oppressed by a spirit of rejection.

"God knows all and He sees all; therefore trust Him and evict the spirit of fear from your thoughts."

t

Chapter Six

Resetting Your Mindset

I beseech you therefore, brethren, by the mercies of God, that ye present your bodies a living sacrifice, holy, acceptable unto God, which is your reasonable service.

2 And be not conformed to this world: but be ye transformed by the renewing of your mind, that ye may prove what is that good, and acceptable, and perfect, will of God. (Romans 12:1-2).

Again, I believe that most of our limitations are in our minds. If we can change the way we think we can change our outcome. The truth is that the enemy can only attack you in your mind and because of that, there is always a battle going on between that which is right and that which is wrong. Most people think themselves out of success before attempting to pursue it. If the enemy can control your thinking he can manipulate your future. In Acts 12:1-2, we are told not to be conformed to the world's system and its way of thinking but to be renewed in the spirit of our mind. I have entitled this chapter, "resetting the Mindset" because I want to show you how to move beyond your limiting beliefs and move towards your destiny.

27 So God created man in his own image, in the image of God created he him; male and female created he them.

28 And God blessed them, and God said unto them, Be fruitful, and multiply, and replenish the earth, and subdue it: and have dominion over the fish of the sea, and over the fowl of the air, and over every living thing that moveth upon the earth. (Genesis 1:27-28)

God created man in His likeness and in His image. To be created in the image of someone or something simply means that the thing created resembles the original. Furthermore, to be created in the likeness of someone or something, means that what was created bares the same ability as the original thing. I said all that to make a point that in Genesis chapter 1, God created the spirit of man and his ability. God is a spirit; therefore if we were created in the likeness and image of God, we are also spirits that possesses the abilities of God. Everything that you see in the natural realm first exists in the mind of God.

And the LORD God formed man of the dust of the ground, and breathed into his nostrils the breath of life; and man became a living soul. (Genesis 2:7).

We see, in this Scripture, that God reaches down to the earth and forms the body of man from the dust of the ground. What I want you to notice is that He then breathes into the nostrils of man the breath of life. So God took the spirit of man, of which He created in His likeness an image, and formed the body of the man from the dust of the ground and breathed the Spirit into the body and man *BECAME* a living soul. This is important to know because it will help you to understand why the enemy is after your mind. Man is a three part creation, spirit, body, and soul. God created the spirit, He also created the earth from which the body came, but notice that the soul *BECAME*. So, it is safe to say that, the enemy cannot have your spirit (which is God's), neither can he have your body (which comes from the earth, and must return), but he can only have which *BECAME* *(your soul).*

Your soul has five components; the mind, emotions, intellect, imagination, and your will. Remember that the desire of the enemy is to derail your destiny and, whenever possible, use your soul to limit your progress. Some people are so emotionally damaged that they are in a state of paralysis and cannot move forward. Many people are intellectually sound but do not possess wisdom; therefore they are limited to only what they know. Still others allow their imagination to move them away from acknowledging God and they choose to believe that all they achieve is a result of their own efforts. Then there are those strong willed people who have their own agenda. Finally, there are natural minded and spiritual minded people. In all of these areas of the soul the enemy launches attacks against you. The hardest thing to do is to reset the mindset of those who have allowed the enemy to establish strongholds. Simple definition of stronghold is that it is a fortress where Satan and his legions of demons hide. The enemy builds walls and establishes strongholds around your beliefs and emotions.

There are strongholds that will hold you strong and cause you to walk in a state of limitation. The enemy is constantly at war with our souls because he knows that our actions originate from our minds. The devil is real and he wants to destroy us. Our minds are his number one battleground and he will release every weapon he has in his arsenal to defeat us. These weapons may include past experiences, disappointments, failures, mistakes, and setbacks. I have good news for you; our weapons are stronger than the weapons of the enemy because our weapons are spiritual.

For the weapons of our warfare are not carnal, but mighty through God to the pulling down of strong holds; Casting down imaginations, and every high thing that exalteth itself against the knowledge of God, and bringing into captivity every thought to the obedience of Christ; (2 Cor 10:4.5)

I declare to you now that no weapon formed against you shall prosper!!!!

It is important to understand that the enemy will always place temptations and distractions before you but your response will determine the outcome. The enemy will always use things that you desire to throw you off track. He will never tempt you with something that you do not want or desire. Remember that we are human but, at the same time, spirit. Our lowest level of existence is the human level, and our highest level of existence is the spiritual level. If we operate at our lower-level, which is a carnal mind set, we will always make decisions and choices that will limit us. Remember that we must choose to believe and confess that God always want the greatest and the best for us.

In Matthew chapter 4, the enemy tried several times to tempt Jesus but He would always remind the devil that the Word of God is more powerful than anything that he can offer. *But he answered and said, It is written, Man shall not live by bread alone, but by every word that proceedeth out of the mouth of God (vs 4).*

Jesus could not be tempted by the devil because His mind was always focused on doing the will of the Father who sent him. The will of God is always found in the Word of God. All temptations presented to us are not contrary to God; they can also be things that we hold on to. For example, when someone is critically or terminally sick I often hear people say "let's just pray for God's will to be done". It is never God's will for us to be sick or in poverty or to be lost. If you want to know what the will of God is, just look in the Word of God and there you will find it. When we work at developing the same mindset in us as was also in Christ Jesus, we become empowered to resist every temptation that the enemy places before us. Throughout our Christian walk we must endeavor to be more like Christ. God created us with the authority to allow the mind of Christ to become active in us.

5. Let this mind be in you, which was also in Christ Jesus:

6. Who, being in the form of God, thought it not robbery to be equal with God:

7. But made himself of no reputation, and took upon him the form of a servant, and was made in the likeness of men:

8. And being found in fashion as a man, he humbled himself, and became obedient unto death, even the death of the cross.

9. Wherefore God also hath highly exalted him, and given him a name which is above every name:

(Philippians 2:5-9)

Our goal, as a Christian, should be to be just like Christ. Jesus was created in the fashion of a man with a spirit, body and soul. The difference in man and Christ is that He was in full control of His soul. He had full control of His mind, will, intellect, emotions and imaginations. Jesus' desire was to do the will of the Father who sent Him and not His own agenda. The Scripture says that you should *LET* the same mindset that Christ had be in you. By virtue of the fact that it says *LET*, indicates that you can do it. You have full function of your mind to cause it to change the way it thinks. So what is the mind of Christ? By studying the New Testament we can extract some of the elements of the mind of Christ.

First of all, Jesus had a mind that was submissive to the Father. Christ was not a self-centered man. He was not stubborn minded; He had a mind of surrender and submission unto Almighty God. He understood that He was the "lamb which was slain from the foundation of the world" according to the book of revelation. He knew that His eternal purpose was to step out of eternity and clothe Himself in humanity and become the sacrifice that would atone for our sins and procure salvation for fallen man. Jesus never argued with God concerning his eternal purpose; indeed He was submissive to the will of God for His life. How submissive are we to the will of God? The measure of our submissiveness is in direct measure to the degree of the mind of Christ that we intentionally develop and purposely allow to be active within us.

Secondly, the mind of Christ is a mind of humility. Jesus never sought to exalt himself but rather gave all glory to God the father. The individual who always seeks to put themselves on a platform to be recognized before everyone is not a person that possesses the mind of Christ. Jesus never took credit Himself for anything He did. In all that He did, He pointed men to God.

Thirdly, Jesus possessed a servant mentality. He did not come to be served but to save and serve others. The life of our Savior was a life of absolute service. He did not seek to do His own will, but the will of the Father. Is this the mind that we possess today? Do you have to be begged and coerced into service? If your answer is yes, you do not possess the mind of Christ. A person who possesses the mind of Christ is someone who is willing to serve.

And lastly, the mind of Christ is a mind of sacrifice. He dedicated His whole life to the service of others. The greatest love Jesus showed was to lay down His life for us. God loved us so much that He gave his only begotten Son to die for us. Jesus loves us so much that He laid down His life that we might receive eternal life. Is it now reasonable for us to love one another so that others may also experience a better life in Christ Jesus? What are you willing to sacrifice in the service of God?

"The hardest thing to do is to reset the mindset of those who have allowed the enemy to establish strongholds."

Chapter Seven

Making the Change

6 Seek ye the LORD while he may be found, call ye upon him while he is near:

7Let the wicked forsake his way, and the unrighteous man his thoughts: and let him return unto the LORD, and he will have mercy upon him; and to our God, for he will abundantly pardon.

8For my thoughts are not your thoughts, neither are your ways my ways, saith the LORD.

9For as the heavens are higher than the earth, so are my ways higher than your ways, and my thoughts than your thoughts. (Isaiah 55:6-9)

Everything changes, nothing stays the same. From the time you were born into this world you begin to change. You were not created to remain a baby that is carried everywhere it goes. God engineered you with legs so that one day you would be able to walk. There are three stages of life through which every human must go;

infancy, adolescence and adulthood. At each stage there are certain changes to our physical body and mental capacity. By the time we reach adulthood, or sometimes even earlier, we will have developed certain beliefs and values that have been embedded within our conscience. Those beliefs and values are a result of our environment, experiences, words of others, and repetitious information that we have heard throughout our lives. The problem is that we have been program with the wrong things. Our minds are like computers. As a matter of fact, the computer was created and designed after the function of the human brain. Constantly things are being downloaded into our brain just as software is downloaded on the computer.

As a man thinks in his heart, so is he: (Prov. 23:7)

In our pre-Christ days we were privy to unrighteous counsel that was downloaded into our minds. But when we come into the knowledge of Jesus Christ and accept Him as our Lord and Savior we must be reprogrammed in your thinking. The new operating system software then becomes the word of God. We must no longer operate using the old mindset but develop a new mindset by applying kingdom principles. I believe that only the word of God can change the way a person think and only the Word of God is able to heal, deliver, and set free. So there must be a change in the system software; and a change in the way we think. If we can change the way we think, we can change what shows up in our lives. The way we think can cause us to be restricted and limited from achieving all that God has for us.

Your thinking will change your beliefs

A good man out of the good treasure of his heart brings forth that which is good; and an evil man out of the evil treasure of his heart brings forth that which is evil. For of the abundance of his heart the mouth speaks. (Luke 6:45).

The word heart refers to the mind. Whatever is in our minds will eventually come out. As a pastor, rather than trying to change someone's appearance, I focus on changing the way that they may have been thinking about themselves. Sometimes it can prove to be very difficult because a person could have been thinking a certain way for long time. If you can change the way a person think about themselves on the inside, it will manifest on the outside. You are a result of what you think and believe. The purpose of the Word of God is to correct all of the erroneous information that has been embedded into your thinking which determines what we believe. Similar to a teacher correcting errors on a paper or essay, the errors in our minds must also be corrected. When corrections are made they must be replaced with the truth of God's word. That is why it is important to join a ministry that provide sound biblical teaching rather than a ministry where emotional theatrics and traditionalisms are practiced. The Bible says, in

"So then faith cometh by hearing, and hearing by the word of God". (Romans 10:17)

If we receive error in our thinking by receiving repetitious information, then we must also receive the truth of God's Word repetitiously. What I mean is that you may not get it the first time so you must constantly and consistently seek after the truth of the Word of God. When I was growing up I would hear people brag about the sickness that was prevalent in their family history. They would say, "high blood pressure runs in our family or diabetes runs in our family "so you will get one of these diseases. If you do not know the Word of God then this way of thinking will be downloaded into your mind. If you get a negative report from the doctor, you have the choice to accept it or reject it through the Word of God. Rather than receive the reports you must remove the negative word and replace it with the Word of God which says, *"Who his own self bare our sins in his own body on the tree that we, being dead to sins, should live unto righteousness: by whose stripes ye were healed. (1 Peter 2:24).* Healing can only take place when you believe that you are authorized to be healed. Receive the word of God, believe it and watch your situation turn around!

Your beliefs will change your expectations

After you change your thinking and your thinking changes your beliefs, your expectations will also change. Many people in the church today have become spectators rather than expectators. Spectators come out to see if something happens, however expectators comes out expecting something to happen. I expect God to move on my behalf in every situation and circumstance. I am not surprised when God does something extraordinary because I expect Him to do it. When your belief system changes it ignites your expectation.

My soul, wait thou only upon God; for my expectation is from him. He only is my rock and my salvation: he is my defense; I shall not be moved. (Ps. 62:5,6)

According to my earnest expectation and my hope, that in nothing I shall be ashamed, but that with all boldness, as always, so now also Christ shall be magnified in my body..... (Phil 1:20)

Once you believe that healing, prosperity and peace of mind belongs to you through the Word of God, you can be bold in your expectation. I don't know about you but I walk in a place of constant expectation that God will move on my behalf every time.

Your expectations will change your attitude

Attitude is often confused with behavior. An attitude is a state of mind, feeling or disposition of an individual. Attitudes cannot be seen until behavior is manifest. The condition of your mind will determine the level of attitude that you have. There are three basic components that contribute to a person's attitude. One is "cognitive component". This pertains to what a person knows and what a person believes. How a person act or reacts to certain things are greatly influenced by his or her own knowledge and experience. The second component is the "effective component". This involves situations that have an effect on a person's life. The last component is the "behavioral component" and this relates to a person's goals or intentions in doing his or her activities. You can have a positive attitude regardless of the situation you find yourself in.

For we have not received the spirit of bondage again to fear; but we have received the Spirit of adoption...And if children, then heirs; heirs of God, and joint-heirs with Christ; (Romans 8:25)

Your attitude should reflect that of someone who is not sick or defeated but rather someone who is already walking in healing and victory. You can begin to boldly proclaim that you have not received the spirit of bondage; the bondage of sickness, disease, poverty and sin but that you are joint heirs with Christ Jesus. Once your expectations have been lifted, your attitude will change.

Your attitude will change your confession

Death and life are in the power of the tongue: and they that love it shall eat the fruit thereof. (Proverbs 18:21).

There is power in the words that we speak. There is a spirit associated with every word that is released which causes it to come to pass. That is why it is important to manage the words that come out of our mouths. It is possible to curse someone and then blessed them with the same tongue. What we speak is usually an indication of the attitude or state of mind in which we are in at the time.

The moment we change our negative attitude to the attitude of Christ there shall be nothing impossible to us. We must see ourselves as God sees us and nothing less. We must understand that our words are important.

A good man out of the good treasure of his heart bringeth forth that which is good; and an evil man out of the evil treasure of his heart bringeth forth that which is evil: for of the abundance of the heart his mouth speaketh. (Luke 6:45).

If you change your attitude, your confession will change also. There are two definitions for confession. Confessions are public validations of your faith or they are public rejections of your faith. In the context of this teaching, I am not referring to the confession of admitting wrongful acts or sin. But I am referring to the speaking forth of faith filled words of expectations. Faith confessions are statement that you make that is in agreement with the word and promises of God. Faith confessions will always have the Holy Spirit associated with them and obligates God to make it come to pass. If you can change what you are saying, you can change what shows up in your life. If the doctor says that you are sick your confession must be that you are healed. If your bank account shows that you are broke, your confession must be, "I am blessed, fully furnished and needing no aid". If you are weak your confession must be, "I am strong". If you feel restricted and limited your confession must be, "I can do all things through Christ who strengthens me". I heard it said, "You have what you said because you said what you have". Meaning that whatever you have in your life is a result of your confession.

For verily I say unto you, That whosoever shall say unto this mountain, Be thou removed, and be thou cast into the sea; and shall not doubt in his heart, but shall believe that

those things which he saith shall come to pass; he shall have whatsoever he saith. (Mark 11:23-24)
This passage of scripture has always been my mantra.
It shows that if you can believe those things that you say (confess) you shall have what you say (confess).

Your confession changes your behavior

Many people are bound by a spirit of limitation because of their resistance to the things of God. The flesh has been taught to desire everything that is contrary to the will of God for your life. Sin always feels good to the flesh and makes it easier to walk after the flesh and resist the Spirit of God. When you begin to confess who you are and whose you are, your flesh must then be subject to your spirit. The enemy knows that if you begin to speak those things that are not as though they were, he cannot hold you and bind you to your flesh. When you begin to confess who you are you will then behave like who you are. For example, if you confess that you are prosperous, you will begin to behave like you are prosperous. If your confession is that you are a Christian, your behavior must reflect that of a Christian.

Submit yourselves therefore to God. Resist the devil and he will flee from you. Draw nigh to God and He will draw nigh to you. (Jam. 4:7,8)

You must submit to God and resist the temptations that the enemy brings through your flesh. To submit to God means to reverence Him, recognize Him, please Him and come under His authority. The Scripture lets us know that the devil can only hang around people who are not submitted to God. It's time to cause the enemy to flee from your presence through your submission to God. Notice, in this scripture, your behavior causes a response. If you submit to God, the enemy will run away. And if you get closer to God, He will get closer to you. It is not that God is far away from you but the closer you get to Him the more He reveals Himself to you.

Your behavior changes your Performance

Remember that you have been created with purpose and given a destiny. Your performance determines your destiny. Your behavior will determine the level of your performance. If an athlete desires to be the best at their sport they must be disciplined and prepare for maximum performance. My son played NCAA football at the University of Louisiana Monroe. During football season the team must show up for practice and do what is required by the coaches. The behavior of the players during practice will determine the level of performance in the game. If the practice is lazy, mediocre and unchallenging, the performance of the game will not be great. But if the behavior of the players is at its maximum potential, it will show in the performance of the team during the game. Your behavior is something that is being displayed constantly; your performance is only for a specific time or event. So we can safely say that your behavior will change your performance.

And we desire that every one of you do show the same diligence to the full assurance of hope unto the end: That you be not slothful, but followers of them who through faith and patience inherit the promises. (Heb 6:11,12)

The word slothful means to be lazy. Laziness produces poor performance. You should wake each morning with purpose and determination to operate in the spirit of excellence concerning the things which God has trusted to you. The Bible tells us that we should be instant in season and out of season or in other words we should always be ready to defend the gospel of Jesus Christ.

Your performance will change your life

Do you need a change in your life? Jesus reminds us over and over that the purpose of His coming was to die for our sins so that we may have life and have it in abundance.

The thief cometh not, but for to steal, and to kill, and to destroy: I am come that they might have life, and that they might have it more abundantly. (John 10:10)

I don't know about you, but I want the life that Jesus came to give me. I also understand that if I want something I must do something. Let us now walk back through the process. When you receive the word of God, it changes what you believe. When you change what you believe, your beliefs change your expectations. You cannot expect something that you do not believe to show up in your life. Once you change your expectations, your expectations will change your attitude. Developing a new attitude will change your confession. Confessions are positive affirmation spoken into the atmosphere. Whatever you confess releases the angels to make it come to pass. Your confessions will change your behavior and your behavior will change your performance. Ultimately, your performance or what you do will change your life.

"The way that you think can cause you to be restricted and limited from achieving all that God has for you."

Chapter Eight

Reversing Your Desires

In this chapter, I want to talk about reversing the desires that limit your progress. There are two types of desires that we will discuss in this chapter; fleshly desires and godly desires. Desire is a craving or longing for something or someone that you believe will give you a certain outcome and satisfaction. When you desire something or someone, just the thought of it will bring excitement into your mind and you will do whatever it takes to get it. Sin comes when we take a perfectly natural desire, longing or ambition and try desperately to fulfill it without God. Anything outside of God becomes a distortion and perversion of the very image of God in which you were created. Man was created with the human nature and spiritual nature. Because you were created in the image of God, who is spirit, your spirit nature is higher than your human nature. We as Christians have a choice to let the Spirit control our decisions or to yield to sinful human desires. The

Apostle Paul urges Christians to stop offering the authority of their decisions to their lower nature (Desiring wealth, position, power, fame, lusts of the flesh and eyes, prideful things) but instead to offer the control of their thinking to spiritual purposes (Desiring His kingdom and righteousness, love, truth, grace, peace, hope faith, evangelism, disciple-making and exhortation). If you're not striving to surrender the control of your mind to righteousness it is inevitable that you will give in to the desires of the flesh. The truth is that we are in a tug-of-war, being constantly pulled in the direction of either our sinful desires or spiritual desires. It is becoming more and more difficult, in the world that we live in, to desire spiritual things. The reason why is that we are being bombarded on a daily basis with marketing, advertisement and even governing laws which causes fleshly desires to be embedded into our thinking. Most commercial advertisement plays on our desire for something that we see that probably does not have anything to do with the product that is being sold. Most commercials will play on your desire for sex and therefore at a sexual content to entice you to purchase the product or service. I want you to understand that desire is not emotions. Desire is usually associated with something that is physical with the hope of both spiritual and physical gratification. When your stomach cramps you desire food but hunger is not an emotion, it is a response to a perceived physical deficit. Only a spiritually mature Christian will have the power to resist the enticements of possessions, security, positions, pleasures or fleshly stimulations. You must not allow these desires to control and order your life. You must deprive your sinful nature of its desires and appetites and asked the Lord to help you feed and strengthen your spiritual nature. Many people are consciously and unconsciously control by their central appetites and too many Christians allow those desires to control their decisions.

I do not consider my life of any <u>account</u> as dear to myself so that I may complete the work God has called me to do." *(Acts 20:24).*

Paul tells us not to allow our bodies to give into the bondage of sin. If you yield to sin, it has the power to ruin you. Most people don't realize that even if you occasionally give in to sin, you are really transferring authority out of the control of the Holy Spirit and giving that authority to your sinful nature. Sin is a slave taskmaster who seeks to destroy, corrupt and ruin its slaves.

If you expect God's blessings, you must have no other master but God. You cannot give a part of your life to God and the other part to your evil desires. He wants all of you. You must yield your mind to righteous desires, purposes and processes, regardless of how difficult they may seem. That is why it is important what you allow to enter into your mind. Whatever enters into your mind the most will determine your desire. Be careful that you do not continuously expose yourself to literature, conversations, philosophies, and programming that may entice you with tempting pleasures. The Power of God is living within you and is constantly helping you to desire what is best for your life. He gives us a boundless power of love for what is good, true and profitable.

The power of God's sustaining grace always exceeds the power of your fleshly desires. The Holy Spirit uses the Word of God to direct our thoughts, rebuke us when we are veering off the righteous way, corrects us by showing us how to realign our thoughts with His thoughts and train our senses to discern good from evil. Your choices will determine the consequences you will live with for all eternity.

Delight thyself also in the LORD: and he shall give thee the desires of thine heart. (Psalms 37:4).

To delight yourself in something means to take great pleasure or satisfaction in. When we delight in the Lord, without hesitation, we put everything in His hands and ultimately trust Him for the end results. I received a great revelation from the Scripture. The word "delight" here means to desire to do the Will of God. The latter part of the Scripture says that God will give you the desires of your heart. It is not saying that God will give you everything that your heart desires but rather that He will place desires in your heart. In other words, if your desire is to please Him, He will put desires in your heart that will break you out of your limitations and propel you into your destiny. If you go on and read the rest of this Psalm you can also see the confidence and the joy it brought to David and also bring to us as we delight in the Lord. In the worst of times, David found delight in the Lord. And likewise in our worst of times, we can find peace in God. I like the way the prophet Isaiah said it, *"Thou wilt keep him in perfect peace, whose mind is stayed on thee: because he trusteth in thee".* *(Isaiah 26:3).*

Finally, brethren, whatsoever things are true, whatsoever things are honest, whatsoever things are just, whatsoever things are pure, whatsoever things are lovely, whatsoever things are of good report; if there be any virtue, and if there be any praise, think on these things. (Philippians 4:8).

We can see, from this Scripture, that you have the ability to manage your thoughts. The Apostle Paul is urging us to take our thinking from a horizontal human realm to a vertical spiritual realm. Remember *"You are the thinker that thinks the thoughts that brings the things"* into your life. Your thoughts will determine your desires and your desires can either move you forward or hold you back.

When your desire is to please God He will place His desires within you. If I look back over my life I really didn't have the desire to be a Pastor or an Apostle and to preach all over the world. But when I made pleasing God my desire, He placed the desire in my heart for international ministry. Without desires we wouldn't accomplish much in life or in the kingdom.

"You must deprive your sinful nature of its desires and appetites and asked the Lord to help you to Feed and strengthen your Spiritual nature."

Chapter Nine

Determination Makes the Difference

"Therefore, my beloved brethren, be ye stedfast, unmoveable, always abounding in the work of the Lord, forasmuch as ye know that your labour is not in vain in the Lord". 1Corinthians 15:58

To be determined is to be resolute, resolved and settle in your mind to continue a course of action regardless of the difficulty until it is complete. Many people are being limited by lack of determination. I want to encourage you to be determined, unmovable, unwavering, and steadfast in the work that you are doing for the Lord because your labor is not in vain.

For I know the thoughts that I think toward you, saith the LORD, thoughts of peace, and not of evil, to give you an expected end. (Jeremiah 29:11).

You must be willing to live your life for Christ regardless of the cost, regardless of what obstacles may come before you, and regardless of the opposition that you will face from your friends, family, and enemies. Jesus offers us life, purpose and a mission that is beyond just existing. There is more to life than just functioning. Extraordinary success is a fruit of extra-ordinary determination. Are you willing to live the life God has prepared for you by putting behind your old ways, old habits, and comfort zones and strive toward the destiny that God has for you?

"I want to know Christ and the power of his resurrection and the fellowship of sharing in his sufferings, becoming like him in his death, and so, somehow, to attain to the resurrection from the dead." (Philippians 3:10-11)

The Apostle Paul begins this passage by describing what he is pursuing. He is not merely focused on the beginning of the race but the end result. When you understand the benefit of the end, it will give you determination go on until you reach it. When there is a lack of clear direction, goals or desired outcome, it is hard to be determined. When I was a soldier in the United States Army, one of the things that each soldier had to do on a biannual basis, was to take a physical training test. The test consisted of push-ups, sit-ups and a two-mile run respectively. The two-mile run was difficult after doing the maximum amount of push-ups and set-ups. Each time I took the test I recognized that the last one quarter-mile was always hard to do. But as I looked ahead and saw the finish line, I begin to think within myself, I have come too far to give up. So I would muster up every ounce of strength that I had left and push my way forward the finish line. I was determined to reach my goal because I understood the benefit of finishing strong. Paul makes it clear that the goal of his life was to know Jesus. He wanted to be a model of who Jesus was and is. Paul's ultimate destination was to end up looking like Jesus and he was determined to get there.

"Not that I have already obtained all this, or have already been made perfect, but I press on to take hold of that for which Christ Jesus took hold of me. Brothers, I do not consider myself yet to have taken hold of it. But one thing I do: Forgetting what is behind and straining toward what is ahead, I press on toward the goal to <u>win the prize</u> for which God has called me heavenward in Christ Jesus."
Philippians 3:12-14

To press towards means to be determined to a known or expected goal or end. You must press on no matter the cost. There is a blessing for those who are determined. Because of determination, Noah and his family were saved from the destruction of the flood. Because of determination, Abraham was called a friend of God. Because of determination, David was able to bring the Ark of the Covenant back into the city of God. Because of determination, Jesus endured the suffering of the cross. Because of determination, Paul was able to say;

"I have fought a good fight, I have finished [my] course, I have kept the faith: Henceforth there is laid up for me a crown of righteousness, which the Lord, the righteous judge, shall give me at that day: and not to me only, but unto all them also that love his appearing". (2 timothy 4:7-8).

"But without faith it is impossible to please Him, for he who comes to God must believe that He is, and that He is a rewarder of those who diligently seek Him." The rewards of God are given to those who diligently seek Him. I believe God wants us to dream a big dream. (Hebrews 11:6)

There is a great reward awaiting those who are determined to seek after the things of God. The enemy does not want you to move forward, but desires to keep you bound by the spirit of limitation. There will be many give up opportunities but determination will move you past them all.

Don't quit

Have you ever been tempted to quit? The challenges of life can either push you towards God or pull you away from God! When my son, Je'Ron, was about five years old, he came home from school and told me something very profound that changed my life. He said, "Daddy, did you know that in order to move to the right you must push to the left, and in order to move the left you must push to the right". He went on to say that if you wanted to go up you must push down and in order to go down you must push up. In other words, he was saying that whichever direction you want to go you must resist the opposite.

Determination is the fuel that will ignite your fire and cause you to resist defeat and replace it with success. Do you have the determination and stamina to go through to the end because you understand the price that was paid at Calvary's cross? God is not seeking perfection in our efforts for He knows that is impossible because we have what is called a sin nature. What God is looking for from us is progress. We must understand that progress is not perfection. We must have something deep inside of us that drives us forward. Those that have obtained success are those who possess an intrinsic force that drives them into that place. You may have had many defeats in your life but now is the time to turn your defeat into determination and finish the course God intentionally designed for you. The first thing you must do is remember what God has done for you and do not forget how He blessed you in the past. Reminisce on the times when you should have been defeated or taken out but God stepped in and dwarfed the plan the enemy. Whenever I feel that something is too hard to endure or it seems that I am going to be defeated, I rejoice in what God has already done in the past. To rejoice means to do over again or to have joy again. The old church people used to say, "When I think of the goodness of Jesus and all that he's done for me, my soul cries out hallelujah thank you for saving me". Understanding your past victories can motivate you for future success.

The second thing is to never question God's plan. There are some things that you must go through but you will not be harmed, you will not be destroyed and you will not be abandoned. Jesus has assured us that He will be with us even unto the end of time. When God created you, He engineered you to be able to handle anything that the enemy throws at you, "when you are walking in His purpose", for God has given you the grace to accomplish every task associated with His plan. Thirdly, you must never settle for less than God's best. As a kingdom citizen, you should always have the best. If God owns everything in the earth then it also belongs to His children. Fourthly, don't worry about what other people think. Now your desire is to please God and not people. You only seek to please those with whom you need approval. But if God approves of you, it doesn't matter what anyone else thinks.

People are limited by what they believe others think about them and they become stuck in a holding pattern, on the runway never able to take off and sore to higher heights. Lastly, don't stay down because of your setback. God will use what was meant for your destruction to be a stepping stone and catalyst for your victory. The difference in a failure and an achiever is that the achiever gets up and is determined to keep moving forward by faith. There will be times when you must encourage yourself. Pick yourself up and get back in the fight. We are designed to be achievers because victory is written in our God-given DNA. God has given us the power to become...

"You must be willing to live your life for Christ regardless of the cost, regardless of what obstacles may come at you, and regardless of the opposition that you will face from your friends, family, and enemies."

Chapter Ten

Self-Discipline

Be sober, be vigilant; because your adversary the devil, as a roaring lion, walketh about, seeking whom he may devour: (1 Peter 5:8-9)

As I stated earlier in this book, the soul is comprised of five parts; the mind, intellect, emotions, imagination and the will. In this chapter I want to deal with discipline because I believe a lack of discipline also empowers the spirit of limitation. If we are going to destroy the spirit of limitation, discipline must be in our strategy. To be discipline is to take a course of action that will lead you to a greater goal while disregarding immediate satisfaction.   There is no need to exercise discipline with something you like or enjoy doing. If you enjoy going to the gym and exercising, then there is no need to discipline yourself to do so. But if you do not like physical training, but you understand the benefits, you will discipline yourself to exercise in order to achieve the desired results. Discipline always requires training which is expected to produce a specific character or pattern of behavior, especially moral or mental improvement. The objective of discipline is to produce controlled behavior or self-control. Discipline is when you give yourself guidelines and boundaries that are not comfortable to you, but will establish the order that you need in your life and cause you to be released from the spirit of limitation.

A disciplined person is a person that establishes goals and is willing to achieve those goals at the expense of his or her immediate comfort. Another word for discipline is self-control or self-discipline. You must learn how to use your will to gain power over your fleshly desires. Discipline always asserts reason over your desires. Self-discipline can be defined as the ability to motivate yourself in spite of your negative emotional state. Willpower, hard work, and persistence are qualities associated with self-discipline.

Self-discipline is the product of persistent will power whereas willpower is the strength and ability to carry out a certain task. Self-discipline is the ability to use willpower routinely and even automatically, as second nature. Let's look at it this way, willpower is the muscle and self-discipline is the structured thought that controls that muscle. One of the enemies to your success is a lack of self-discipline.

"But the fruit of the Spirit is love, joy, peace, patience, kindness, goodness, faithfulness, gentleness and self-control. Against such things there is no law." (Galatians 5:22-23)

Each of the different characteristics of the Fruit of the Spirit focuses on how we respond to God and how we treat other people. Joy and faithfulness are expressed vertically while peace, patience, kindness, goodness and gentleness bear directly on how we interact with others. Relationship with God should always be expressed in a vertical dimension whereas your relationship with others should always be expressed in a horizontal dimension. Love is the only fruit that can be expressed both vertically and horizontally.

At the end of the list is Self-control, which always has to do with your relationship with yourself. This characteristic of a Christ-follower seems to focus more on self instead of on relationships with other people. You can exercise self-control when you are the only person in the house. In fact, sometimes the hidden, private moment when no one else is looking is precisely when you need self-control the most. If you properly exercise the fruit of self-control, it will benefit those around you as well.

Most of the things that are limiting you are not external but internal. If you want to be released from the bondage of your desires, you must learn how to exercise self-control. In the NIV translation of the Bible you will see the word temperance which is the same as self-control. It comes from the word "strength" and means, "one who holds himself in." Sometimes that is easier said than done because while "self-control" is a good translation of the Greek word, it's a bit deceiving because we all know that we can't control ourselves simply through our own willpower or self-determination. If that was the case then there would be no need for the power of God to work in you. There is a conundrum and a dilemma that's working inside of us and the Apostle Paul, in this passage, so eloquently states it.

14 For we know that the law is spiritual: but I am carnal, sold under sin.15 For that which I do I allow not: for what I would, that do I not; but what I hate, that do I. 16 If then I do that which I would not, I consent unto the law that it is good. 17 Now then it is no more I that do it, but sin that dwelleth in me. 18 For I know that in me (that is, in my flesh,) dwelleth no good thing: for to will is present with me; but how to perform that which is good I find not. 19 For the good that I would I do not: but the evil which I would not, that I do. 20 Now if I do that I would not, it is no more I that do it, but sin that dwelleth in me. 21 I find then a law, that, when I would do good, evil is present with me. 22 For I delight in the law of God after the inward man: 23 But I see another law in my members, warring against the law of my mind, and bringing me into captivity to the *law of sin which is in my members. ^{24} O wretched man that I am! who shall deliver me from the body of this death? ^{25} I thank God through Jesus Christ our Lord. So then with the mind I myself serve the law of God; but with the flesh the law of sin.*

The Apostle Paul is puzzled and wrestling within himself as to why he cannot exercise self-control. If the Apostle Paul had difficulty exercising self-control, then it is safe to say that you and I do as well. You must realize that you can do nothing outside of God. If you are to bring your flesh under subjection, you must submit totally to the Spirit of God.

26 I therefore so run, not as uncertainly; so fight I, not as one that beateth the air:
27 But I keep under my body, and bring it into subjection: lest that by any means, when I have preached to others, I myself should be a castaway. (1 Corinthians 9:26-27)

We can get a clearer meaning of self-control from Paul's extended discussion of his ministry in 1 Corinthians 9. In this passage, Paul contrasts exercising control over his body with running "aimlessly" in verse 26. He argues that athletes exercise self-control because they have a clearly defined purpose or goal. When you have a clearly defined purpose and goal, you cannot afford to be distracted by every passion and desire that comes along. What looks like self-control is actually the result of letting the Holy Spirit take control. Biblically speaking, self-control means to walk by the Spirit, under the Lordship of Jesus Christ.

"A disciplined person is a person that establishes goals and is willing to achieve those goals at the expense of his or her immediate comfort".

Chapter Eleven

Limiting God

There will be many doors of opportunities that will be placed before you to walk through but it is possible that you can miss those opportunities. Whenever you miss those opportunities, you limit what God can do in your life thereby; limiting what Christ is able to do through you. I believe that no one wants to settle for second best but want to be all that they can be in Christ Jesus. It is important to maintain a good positive attitude because your attitude can either help or hinder you. An attitude of faith can unleash the miraculous Power of God, but unbelief can block that power.

Mark 6:5-6 tells us: "Now He could do no mighty work there, except that He laid His hands on a few sick people and healed them. And He marveled because of their unbelief." (NKJV)

When Jesus went back to his home town, unfortunately, there was a climate of unbelief and wrong attitudes that limited the work of God. Your unbelief can limit God, not because He is unwilling or powerless but because you choose not to believe Him. As the story unfolds, we find Jesus coming back to His home town. As He and His disciples were there, He began to teach in the synagogue on the Sabbath day. As usual, His teachings were brilliant. He taught as one who had authority, and not as the Scribes. He gave them insight into God's Word and they were astonished. But after all of that, they said He is just a "carpenter" who left town. He is just the son of Mary. He is just the brother of James, Joseph, Judas and Simon. We know His sisters. Jesus was amazed at their lack of faith and because of their unbelief many returned to their homes sick, lame, blind and demon-possessed.

When we limit God in our lives, we are not the only ones who suffer loss. The message here is simple: Unbelief limits the power of God. Jesus could only do a few miracles there because the spirit of limitation was empowered by unbelief. The Power of God was held back because people refused to believe. The cause of their unbelief was their limited view of Jesus. They were limited by what they could see, by what they know and what they could understand. Who they had before them was the Messiah, the Son of God but who they saw was the carpenter, the son of Mary. Their limited views kept them from seeing who Jesus really was. They had stereotyped Jesus and could not see beyond their own natural understanding of the carpenter's son who grew up in their own community. A distorted view of Jesus, who He is or what He can do, will rob you of your faith.

You limit what God can do because of your limited viewpoint. You must learn to see beyond your own natural understanding. We do not have to understand how a thing works in order to receive it by faith and to receive the benefit it brings to us. I may not understand electricity, but I'm not going to live in the dark. Thank God that a lot of things are possible for us beyond our ability to understand them. The Bible teaches that we should walk by faith and not by sight. Walking by sight limits what God can do. And though we have a tendency to want to understand the end from the beginning, sometimes, like Abraham, we must leave where we are and journey to a place of which God has not yet show us. Sometimes we must respond to Jesus' command "Only believe." The consequence for unbelief is that the power of God is limited. You must understand that God is no less powerful because of your unbelief but rather, He has designed that power to be used in response to faith. The Power of God is designed to be released as we trust Him by faith. When the Power of God is locked up through unbelief, the Blessings of God are limited. Unbelief not only locks up the power of God, it also limits the provision of God. We limit Him when we look at familiar things and situations choose not to believe that God can do anything about it. We limit God when we choose to believe that God can't use us to do anything great. Today God wants to bless us with more so don't limit Him by your unbelief. Trust Him and keep doing what is right!

14 If my people, which are called by my name, shall humble themselves, and pray, and seek my face, and turn from their wicked ways; then will I hear from heaven, and will forgive their sin, and will heal their land. (2 Chronicles 7:14)

Confess your faults one to another, and pray one for another, that ye may be healed. The effectual fervent prayer of a righteous man availeth much. (James 5:16)

The Bible tells us that faith come through hearing the word of God. In the same manner, if faith comes by hearing then doubt and unbelief also comes by hearing. If you are going to be release from the disease of unbelief, your medicine is the Word of God. You must also develop a strong prayer life. As we see in the previous Scripture the Power of God shows up when prayer is released. Many times what shows up and how it shows up may not be what you want but just remember that all things work out for the good of those that are in Christ Jesus. I like the way James explain it, if your prayer is effectual and fervent it will bring much into manifestation.

But thou art holy, O thou that inhabitest the praises of Israel. (Psalm 22:3)

Not only can you limit the Power of God by your lack of prayer, but you can also limit God through a lack of praise and worship. It is evident throughout Scripture that the presence of God always shows up in midst of praise. To inhabit means to dwell in the midst of. So when you begin to praise God, He literally dwells in the midst of your praise and worship. Isn't it good to know that if you want God to show up in the middle of your circumstances, situations and challenges that all you have to do is believe and praise Him in the middle of it.

Sin will also limit what God can do in your life. God is a perfect spiritual being and He cannot be in the presence of sin. Let me explain it like this; the natural habitat of fish is to be in water. If a fish is out of water for an extended period of time, it cannot survive because of the environment. God is perfect and everything around Him is perfect. Before the fall of Lucifer everything in heaven was in order and perfect. Only after rebellion entered into the heart of Lucifer, did sin appear. Theoretically, sin does not exist but it is, rather, the absence of obedience. Evil only exists where there is an absence of good. Scientifically, cold does not exist but it is only the absence and heat.

For all have sinned, and come short of the glory of God;
(Romans 3:23)

This passage of Scripture is often used by many to justify sin. When someone is caught up in sin you can often hear people say, "Well, all have sinned and come short of the Glory of God", as if that is an excuse for sin. What I believe this Scripture is saying is that God wants His glory to show through us but when we are in sin, it limit the Power of God from making us instruments of His glory.

2 Cor. 3:18 – "that we can be mirrors that brightly reflect the glory of the Lord. And as the Spirit of the Lord works within us, we become more and more like Him, and reflect His glory even more."

"You must understand that God is no less powerful because of your unbelief. It is simply that He has designed that power to be used in response to faith."

Chapter Twelve

Destroying the Spirit of Limitations

But ye are a chosen generation, a royal priesthood, an holy nation, a peculiar people; that ye should shew forth the praises of him who hath called you out of darkness into his marvellous light; (1 Peter 2:9)

There are two forces always at work; darkness and light. The bible states that there is a kingdom of darkness and a kingdom of light that coexist. Those who have not accepted Jesus Christ as Lord and Savior are still part of the kingdom of darkness. But those who have accepted Christ have been called into light, which is the kingdom of God. If you are saved that means that you are chosen, you are royalty, you have been bought with the blood of Jesus and you should give all praises to God. If you have not accepted Christ as your Lord and Savior, according to Romans 10:9, you must confess with your mouth the Lord Jesus, and believe in your heart that God has raised him from the dead. Receive your salvation and enter into the kingdom of God. Darkness is always restrictive and limiting but light will illuminate your path to destiny. When a person is in darkness their sight is limited and their movement is restricted. They run into things that cannot be seen beforehand. It is possible as a Christian that we may find ourselves in some dark situations but God has given us His word that will guide us through the dark times of our lives. When I was in the United States Army on training exercises and deployments, each soldier would be issued a set of night vision goggles that would enable us to see at night, even in total darkness. In the early 90's while deployed in Saudi Arabia in preparation for operation Desert Storm, I learned quickly that it was impossible, or at least very difficult, to operate in total darkness. I had to rely heavily on my night vision goggles in order to be able to see and accomplish every task assigned to me, regardless of the time of day or night. When you are in darkness it is difficult to see where God wants you to go according to His plan. But I thank God that even when I was in the midst of darkness the light of His word always guided my footsteps.

Thy word is a lamp unto my feet, and a light unto my path. (Psalm 119:105)

Notice here that it says "Path" which indicates movement. When your destiny is considered risky by the enemy, you will face attacks. Many people wonder why they are faced with so many fierce battles, trials and tribulations. They should rejoice because it means there is something in their lives worth contending for. When you are anointed with purpose and destiny the enemy will rage against you with more intensity. Although our victory was declared over 2,000 years ago, the enemy still wants to contend with us. The greater the vision assignment you have, the greater the opposition you will face. To whom much is given much is required.

Overcoming Obstacles and Setbacks

The devil and his demons are always at work putting obstacles in our paths. Their purpose is to throw us off track and to deter us from moving forward. But I want us to look at obstacles in a different way. Obstacles cause our minds to open up and become more flexible. They cause us to think in new ways in which we have never done before. Obstacles cause us to expand our perspective and become more attentive. The strategy of opposing combat forces is to slow the progress of their opponents by placing obstacles before their path. The purpose of these obstacles is to restrict movement, confuse the opponent and exhaust resources. I learned firsthand during military training and combat exercises where we would place roadblocks, barbed wire and man-made dirt mounds in the path to limit the advancement of the opposing force.

An obstacle can appear to be ending point but for believers it is really the beginning of a new condition that will allow us to think at a higher level. The enemy will always provide "give up" opportunities. Obstacles are meant to cause us to think that our goal isn't meant for us but what they really do is revel more to us. The enemy wants us to give up but I encourage you to keep pressing forth.

There must be a paradigm shift in our mindset in order to breach these obstacles. To shift our thinking, we must start to see an obstacle as a friend. Obstacles and set backs are actually partners with us to make us move proactively towards our goals. You must use every adversity, disappointment, problem, setback and challenge to push you into your place of destiny and purpose.

Many people have allowed the enemy to set obstacles in their way which causes them to become stagnant and unproductive. Remember that limitation is a spirit and the only place it can work is in your mind. When the shift takes place you are creating new dynamics and parameters in your mindset. When you change the dynamics you change the condition of your situation. Then the help you need will respond to your condition.

Before you can become wealthy your thinking about money must change then it will show up in your life. I heard a preacher say it this way, "You are the thinker that thinks the thoughts that bring the things".

For verily I say unto you, That whosoever shall say unto this mountain, Be thou removed, and be thou cast into the sea; and shall not doubt in his heart, but shall believe that those things which he saith shall come to pass; he shall have whatsoever he saith. (Mark 11:23)

New problems and challenges thrive on the environment that it currently exists in. If you change your conditions, the ecology of your problem must also change. So I encourage you to build a new set of conditions around your obstacles. Speak to every obstacle that lie in your way and tell it to move in the name of Jesus. When we speak those things that be not as though they were we release faith that will cause us to change our conditions. The spirit of limitation can only be destroyed, in your life, by you and only you.

Sited Readings.

http://www.mindtools.com/pages/article/fear-of-uccess.htm.

http://ww w.qwhatis.com/what-is-attitude/